Findability: Why Search Engine Optimization is Dying, and the 21 New Rules of Content Marketing for 2013 and Beyond

by Randy Milanovic

Table of Contents

4 ..... **Search Engine Optimization is Dying Right Before Our Eyes...**

6 ..... Why We're Looking at the Beginning of the End of Search Optimization

9 ..... Smarter Search and Smarter Searchers

12 ... It's Not All About Search Anymore, Anyway

15 ... One Thing to Mention Before We Move On

17 ... Findability: What it Takes to Stand Out Going Forward

19 ... **The New Rules of Content Marketing**

20 ... Rule #1: Treat Keywords Like Hot Sauce

21 ... Rule #2: Have a Voice (or Brand) That Customers Can Identify

23 ... Rule #3: Build Trust With Transparency

24 ... Rule #4: Make the Most of a Great Idea With Multiple Formats

26 ... Rule #5: Headlines are Everything

27 ... Rule #6: Use the News

29 ... Rule #7: You Can't Stock the Cupboards Until You Take Out the Trash

30 ... Rule #8: Don't Just Post... Engage!

32 ... Rule #9: Invite Yourself to Someone Else's Party Once in a While

Randy Milanovic

33 ... Rule #10: Remember That Great Content Invites Links

35 ... Rule #11: Build Your Content From an Ongoing Plan

37 ... Rule #12: The Best Inspiration Comes From Several
Different Sources

38 ... Rule #13: Quality is as Important as Quantity

40 ... Rule #14: Quantity Still Matters

41 ... Rule #15: Take Your Time

43 ... Rule #16: Stop Buying Content From the Bargain Bin

44 ... Rule #17: Know Your Biggest Content Marketing
Enemy

46 ... Rule #18: Use One Piece of Content to Promote
Another

47 ... Rule #19: Recycle Your Greatest Hits

48 ... Rule #20: Always Ask the Key Question About
a Piece of Content

50 ... Rule #21: Use Your Content to Turn Searchers,
Readers, and Fans Into Buyers

52 ... **Where Are All the Tags, Keywords,
and Technical Details?**

54 ... Putting All the Pieces Together

56 ... One Final Word...

Randy Milanovic

Search Engine Optimization is Dying Right Before Our Eyes...

If you own or manage a business that gets at least some of its customers from the Internet (and what kind of business these days doesn't?), then you need to be aware of two important trends that seem to contradict each other, but actually work together.

First, it's becoming more important than ever to be easily found on the Internet, especially on important "hubs," like Google, Facebook, Twitter, and YouTube. Put together, these hubs account for billions upon billions of visitors every month. More importantly, though, they tend to be the starting point for new business relationships. That is, if someone wants to buy something but doesn't know exactly what it is, or where they are going to get it, they are very likely to look for information and/or advice on at least one of those sites.

Second, however, traditional search engine optimization – the set of tools and techniques most companies have used for the past decade to make themselves easier for customers to find – is dying right in front of us. It doesn't work as well as it used to, and the chances are good that very soon it won't work at all.

That means change is going to be a necessity for companies, organizations, and websites that want to survive. Doing things the same way that they've been done in the past is going to get you nowhere (or worse). In this short e-book, we are going to show you why that is and what you can do about it.

Before we move into that, though, let us give you a quick word of assurance: Even though search engine optimization as you know it might be going away, something better is taking its place. And, if you can be ready as that happens, you're going to benefit in the new world of content marketing and leave your competitors wondering just how you did it.

Randy Milanovic

Why We're Looking at the Beginning of the End of Search Optimization

To understand why search optimization isn't going to work anymore, we need to take a (very brief) look at where it came from, and how we got to the point we're at today.

Although most of us take Google and the other search engines for granted now, take a moment and consider why it is they even exist at all: because the Internet is too big, and growing too quickly, for people to always have a good idea of what it is they are searching for. After all, if we all knew where to find the information we needed at any given time, we wouldn't have to bother with a middleman to help us weed out the results.

We don't, though, and so we rely on search engines to scour the Internet and deliver listings that will help us find the appropriate destination. If you can remember that this is a search engine's real job, then you can start to see why they are changing so quickly out of necessity.

From the first days, search engines have followed a fairly simple process for determining what those results we all need should look like: They "crawl" the

Internet with automated pieces of software called spiders, moving from one link to the next. When they find a new page, they look through it to find the important words, phrases, and other information that tells them what the page is really about. This system is largely automated, of course, so it isn't usually a personal decision to favor one item over another. [1]

In a perfect world, that kind of program would be enough: Software would scour the Web on a regular basis, find the right pages for the right people, and all would be well. Unfortunately, we don't live in that world – we live in one where businesses, careers, and profits are riding on search engine listings, and so things started to change pretty quickly.

As the Web continued to grow and search engines became more and more popular, marketers found the main ingredients for a favorable search listing. It wasn't long before they were coming up with all kinds of ways to stack the odds in their favor, using things like fake links, pages that repeated the same word or phrase hundreds of times, and so on.

These kinds of tactics made a certain amount of sense for individual companies, but were the Internet equivalent of dumping trash into the ocean. Once everyone

Randy Milanovic

started using them, it became very difficult for actual people to find quality results. Instead, they were far more likely to find sites that were simply the most optimized for a particular search phrase.

Since actual experts and human beings tend not to write in incredibly predictable, repetitive ways, the problem got worse and worse: The best things on the Web were getting harder to find, and the worst kinds of pages were becoming ubiquitous, simply because the "dumping" approach worked.

That, in a nutshell, leads us to where we are today. Although things have changed a little here and there, the basic approach to search engine optimization has been to emphasize keywords, links, and a few technical details, in the hopes that searchers would eventually find your site and decide to become customers.

That's not good for searchers, though, which means it's not good for Google and the other search engines, either. The more low-quality results they display, the easier it is for searchers to decide to look for what they need elsewhere. And, if enough people go elsewhere, advertisers will follow them. Given that reality, the focus at Google and the other search engines always has to be on delivering the best, most accurate search results possible. It's becoming clear that focusing on keywords and links isn't going to be the best way to do that going forward.

Smarter Search
and Smarter Searchers

With over-optimized websites clogging the rankings on search engines, making it tougher for real people to find what they're looking for, two predictable things started to happen: First, Google and its competitors are changing the ways they compile and display results; and second, Internet users themselves are beginning to act differently online.

In the first case, Google's desire to keep reinventing itself is all about attaining market share. If people keep using Google by an 8 or 9 to 1 margin over other search engines, the company can keep attracting huge advertising revenues and move toward world domination and other long-term goals. In order to make that happen, though, some big shifts have been required, and will be needed on an ongoing basis.

Rather than simply looking at things like keywords and links, the company is now starting to consider other factors about your business website more intently, such as:

- The age of your website
- How often you add new pages, articles, and content

- The ease or difficulty of finding information with your navigation structure

- How long visitors tend to spend on your site

- Whether you seem to be trying to "cheat" the system with too much optimization

- The quality and originality of what's on your pages

- Whether you have lots of advertising, and especially affiliate links and ads

- How trustworthy you and your company seem, based on other outside sources

In other words, they are doing more to look at your site the way an actual person would, and making common-sense judgments that go far beyond a few links and meta-tags. What's more, they are ignoring or even penalizing companies that are going too far to influence their ranking. Does that mean they hate you when you're just trying to stand out? Of course not – it just means they know what everyone else does: that no one likes finding over-optimized pages when they're looking for real products, advice, or information.

This process will go on and on over time, and no one can predict exactly what Google and the other engines will look for five years from now. But, you can avoid the pain and suffering that a lot of website owners feel every time an algorithm changes by simply applying a bit of common sense. In other words, you don't have to read the minds of the engineers at Google, or follow every single minute shift in search engine weighting or strategy. That's because you already know where they are headed, because you know what they want to achieve. If you simply build a website that people want to find, you'll always be on the right side of the equation, because Google will be developing better ways to keep finding you, instead of the other way around.

Randy Milanovic

It's Not All About Search Anymore, Anyway

At the same time that Google and the other search engines are looking for new ways to mathematically determine the most informative and trustworthy sites on the Internet, actual people are taking matters into their own hands as well. Instead of simply turning to Google for everything, they are combining what they find there with other information, or skipping search engines altogether.

In most cases, they are looking to social media sites like Facebook, Twitter, and LinkedIn instead. Although none of these are designed specifically for search purposes, they offer something that Google and its competitors have a hard time matching: advice and recommendations from people you already know and trust, or who are very similar to you. They bring the human element back into the equation.

That's important because, no matter how strong search engine algorithms become, they are really just complicated equations and formulas. Social media sites, on the other hand, are run by feedback, opinion, and interaction. So, it doesn't matter how optimized a company's site is; if people don't like their products and prices, they'll never develop a strong social following. For someone looking for the right product or service, that might mean more time spent searching, but also more trustworthy results.

This ongoing change in social media as a source of information, and not just a person-to-person contact, could end up being incredibly important to Internet marketers. In the short term, it certainly forces businesses of all sizes to maintain profiles on sites like Facebook and LinkedIn, and to ensure that they are taking advantage of them to interact with customers and prospects.

In a bigger sense, the major search engines have seen the power of social sites and are working to integrate some of the same features into their own results. That means the information in your social profiles, and possibly your posts and updates, is likely to be indexed by Google. There is still some debate about whether (or how) social content will be displayed in search results going forward, but Google and its competitors seem to be taking the size of your social network, the frequency of your posts, etc., into account to see how "important" and "trusted" you are. After all, the opinions of real people carry a lot more weight than a few links or keywords.

The bottom line in all of this is that you can't just rely on search engines to help customers find you anymore. Trying to follow the same strategies that worked just a few years ago can put you out of business now. It's time to think bigger, and to do better.

Randy Milanovic

One Thing to Mention Before We Move On...

To this point, we haven't said much about YouTube, even though it's one of the most important sites on the Internet, and there are important advantages to posting marketing videos online.

Some people think of YouTube as a social media site. To others, it's "the world's second-largest search engine," because it's owned by Google and attracts an estimated one out of every two Internet users each month (at the time of this writing, and that number is only increasing). Regardless of how you look at the site itself, though, here are some important reasons to make the most of it:

Video can add a different dimension to what you have to say, and some people very much prefer it to plain text or images.

Online video clips can be used to show off your products, demonstrate how a service works, share customer testimonials, and accomplish other tasks with an in-person, "face-to-face" feeling that's hard to duplicate otherwise.

Video clips on the Internet, and especially on YouTube, are displayed separately in search engine results, and can be posted to social profiles. That means they can pull "double duty" as marketing tools.

It's getting less expensive to produce Internet marketing videos all the time.

So, even though a detailed guide on working with Internet video clips should be a topic for its own e-book, know that taking the content strategies we'll be getting to in a moment and adapting them to video format is a great way to achieve a bigger reach, quickly and affordably.

Findability: What it Takes to Stand Out Going Forward

In this new world of Internet marketing, it's not about being "optimized," but being "easy to find." That sounds like a subtle difference, but it couldn't be more profound.

One has to do with page tags, keywords, and trying to manipulate incoming links; the other is about generating interesting ideas, starting discussions, and being a prominent voice in your market or industry. It's the difference between screaming nonsense through a microphone and having journalists come to you for an expert opinion.

Going forward, the smartest companies are going to engage in a new kind of content marketing. That's a term that has taken a hit in the past decade or so, as businesses have come to associate the phrase with cheap, nonsensical articles that are jammed with keywords and are mass-produced to go on low-quality "distribution hubs" that no one bothers to read, anyway. That's unfortunate, because the real roots of content marketing, in its best form, go back to the earlier days of public relations.

For a long time, businesses have known that advertising is expensive, but positive PR and "buzz" are priceless. Placing an ad in a major newspaper could generate exposure, for example, but having a well-written column or opinion piece in the same space is worth a whole lot more. That's because people might glance at ads, but they read informative pieces. Why settle for a half second of attention when you could have customers reading your ideas for minutes at a time, saving them, passing them on, and learning about your expertise in the process?

That can only happen when you have really insightful and well-expressed ideas to share, of course, and that's the kind of content marketing you'll have to focus on going forward – not just putting words on the screen, but generating thought-provoking posts, articles, tweets, pictures, and videos that are so compelling they are virtually impossible to ignore.

The 21 New Rules
of Content Marketing

That brings us to the biggest question of all: How do you create that kind of content... and make potential customers start seeking you out in the process?

There isn't any set formula that's always going to work, or that you can generically apply from one business or industry to the next. Content marketing is both an art and a science, something intricate, delicate, and powerful all at once. In the next section, I am going to share with you some of the simplest and most effective ways to make your content stronger. Use them as a springboard to develop your own content marketing plan, or to have a professional help create one for you.

Randy Milanovic

Rule #1:
Treat Keywords
Like Hot Sauce

As you might've guessed from what we've already shared, marketers are in a bit of a Catch-22 going forward when it comes to keywords. On the one hand, they are still necessary and important if people are going to find you on the Internet. But on the other hand, there is a much bigger risk of having too many keywords on your pages than too few.

Make no mistake: It's becoming increasingly apparent that penalties for "over-optimized" websites are here, and the effects are getting stronger and stronger. Google and the other search engines don't want to see sites written for search engine spiders. More importantly, though, is that real people – the men and women whom you're ultimately going to try to convince to buy from you – don't like them either.

The best answer is to treat search keywords like you would a powerful hot sauce. Used sparingly, they can enhance the "flavor" of your website, posts, and social material, making them easier for buyers to find. Drown your pages in too much, though, and you ruin the entire effect.

There probably aren't ever going to be any hard and fast rules that will always apply, but a good guideline is to use an important keyword once in your title and (at most) a couple of times later on the page. That's enough to make sure your content gets noticed, but not enough to invoke search penalties or annoy readers.

Rule #2:
Have a Voice (or Brand)
That Customers Can Identify

With all of the changes going on in Internet marketing, attracting new customers and readers can be difficult. So, it only makes sense to be sure you don't let them slip away. That's where having a strong and unique voice (a brand) comes into play.

If you think about most major national ad campaigns, they tend to feature a distinct message and tone. Some are funny, some are serious, etc., but they all have a kind of theme and personality that shows up on television spots, magazine ads, popular Web pages, and more, week after week. That consistency creates a subtle impression in a buyer's mind. It also gives them the chance to "look forward" to new messages or installments.

You don't have to have a massive advertising agency on your side to build that same kind of focus into your content marketing. All you have to have is a sense of who your audience is, and who you want to be to them (or how you want your business to be perceived). Then, you simply ensure that the new content you develop fits into that model.

Naturally, you want to ensure that the voice you're cultivating strikes the right balance between appropriate and attention-grabbing. For example, a local bakery can get away with a lot more than a cancer research center. The point isn't to be over the top, but to know that readers, followers, and customers should be able to expect a certain kind of tone from you. That way, they can learn to recognize your brand, feel more attached to it, and keep coming back to your messages again and again.

Rule #3:
Build Trust
With Transparency

Several studies have shown that the biggest obstacle to winning customers online is often trust. Because of the anonymous nature of the Internet, and the huge number of online scams that have been reported on over the years, people just don't trust businesses to do what they say they will, or even actually be who they say they are.

The easiest way around this problem is to simply build trust with buyers by being as transparent as you possibly can. When you post content, let them know who wrote or compiled it, what changes have been made from one version to the next, how the information has been sourced, and so on.

You could even take things further and let them know a little bit about yourself or your company – where you come from, what your biggest values are, and even why you're posting content in the first place. It's no secret that content marketing is designed to help the business make money, so being up front about it can actually help you win credibility.

Even if this weren't good marketing sense, the push toward transparency and accountability has already begun online. Google is tracking "authors" and ranking them in the same way that it does websites with page rank. Social media platforms are using verifiable info to make sure that members actually exist and have the credentials they say they do.

These are steps in the right direction, both because they protect the public from being taken in, and because transparency helps to build trust. If you want buyers to pay attention to your content, don't leave them in the dark about what it really is, or where it's really coming from.

Rule #4:
Make the Most of a Great Idea
With Multiple Formats

It doesn't take a lot of experience in content marketing to realize that great ideas don't just fall from the sky. They are out there, but finding them takes work, patience, and a lot of brainstorming. Given the effort involved, it makes sense to get the most mileage out of each gem by producing it in multiple formats.

For example, one moment of inspiration might lead to a brilliant blog post. But, you can often repackage the same thought – or take a new angle on it, go into more detail, or update it – and come away with another concept for a tweet, a LinkedIn discussion, or even an e-book like this one.

Although thinking of your ideas this way certainly helps you expand your content marketing plan, it's good for the customers you want to reach as well. That's because different people have different preferences; while some would rather read your ideas, others would prefer to see a video clip with human faces or animation.

Additionally, having your idea expressed in different formats makes them easier to find. Remember, it isn't just about Google anymore; the potential customer could just as easily come across your business while searching through LinkedIn or YouTube, or asking about recommendations on Facebook. It's important that they be able to find you in each.

It also helps if you promote your content from one format to the next. In other words, you can send tweets when you have a blog post you really want to share, or use Facebook to drive contacts to your LinkedIn profile, and vice versa. The point is to always look for great ideas, and then find multiple ways to express them when you do.

Rule #5:
Headlines are Everything

That might be a slight exaggeration – having a great headline with terrible content to back it up is a bad idea – but before any article, post, or video can have an impact, you have to convince someone to spend time on it first. That's where headlines come in.

There are any number of ways to come up with fantastic headlines and titles, but the very best is to ask a question or evoke an immediate emotional response in a potential customer. Also, list-type titles naturally pique curiosity. It's even better if you can tie them into current events and trends, or make it clear that your content is time-sensitive.

Put these ideas together, and you can come up with attention-grabbing headlines like: "5 Reasons Search Engine Optimization Will be Completely Different Next Year," "The One Rule Of Social Media Marketing Almost Every Small Business Is Breaking," and "Is Now the Right Time to Completely Change Your Email Marketing Focus?" These are just examples, of course, but you can see how each one creates a question in a reader's (or viewer's) mind that they almost can't bear to not know the answer to.

If you find that you're struggling with headlines, check out some of your favorite magazines and websites. Even if they don't apply to your industry, the styles they use to "hook" you into a piece of writing can help serve as an inspirational starting point. Change the focus to your industry, think about adding in a key search term or phrase, and you are well on your way to a winning title.

When it comes to having your content noticed, nothing beats a great headline, so go through as many versions as you need to in order to find a winner.

Randy Milanovic

Rule #6:
Use the News

An easy way to stay current, catch attention, and make your content more valuable is by matching your idea to some current event or trend. In other words, by watching what's going on with the news, you can sometimes develop topics and angles that make your content more edgy or compelling than it would have been otherwise.

In our business, we have used this concept to "piggyback" off of lots of news items, including popular movies, sporting events, political figures, and so on. One of our most well-received pieces of content explains how a popular TV character would have dealt with an Internet marketing challenge (and subsequently gotten it wrong). It works so well because we took something that people were talking about anyway and placed it in the context of our industry. The resulting content explained some valuable points, got people thinking, and created a bit of buzz for our company.

You can do the same. Just pay attention to what's going on (especially in the popular media) and see how you can use it to relate to your own content marketing topics or ideas. At first, it might take some time and creative thinking for you to come up with a concept that works, but it's a skill that develops quickly.

You don't want all of your posts or updates to be tied to current events, since that could make your content marketing seem gimmicky. But, by taking advantage of what's going on in the news once in a while, you can attract readers who might have otherwise skipped over what you have to say.

Rule #7:
You Can't Stock the Cupboards Until You Take Out the Trash

Before your content marketing plan can truly succeed, you might have some spring cleaning to do. That's because, if you're trying to attract attention via search engines and social media sites, there is a good chance you have engaged in some of the tactics we talked about in the first section.

Now, you have to clean up the litter around your own property before you can put something better in its place.

How far will you have to go? That depends on how bad the damage is. If you have a few low-quality articles on your site that are still getting good page views, then you might be able to get away with simply cleaning them up, making some edits, and leaving them in place. If your site is packed with spam-type, keyword-stuffed pages with overused tags and "junk" content, however, you might want to clear these away, create a new navigation structure, and take other steps to make your site friendlier to people instead of search spiders.

This is a different activity from "disavowing" low-quality backlinks, which can be just as important, but require a bit more time and technical expertise. Still, it's best to do both at the same time if your website seems untrustworthy to search engines and customers.

Of course, if you have problems with existing content, you've probably been watching the incoming traffic to, and conversion performance from, your business website suffer for a while, anyway. So, don't wait any longer to turn things around – start to clear away what isn't needed so you can put better, more visible content in its place.

Randy Milanovic

Rule #8:
Don't Just Post...Engage!

Probably the easiest way to tell poor content from great content is simply to watch what kinds of shares, responses, and other feedback are generated. When an idea is truly unique, or at least put into a high-quality post or video, customers, colleagues, and others are going to chime in. When it's just "more of the same old Internet marketing material," on the other hand, no one cares… and so no one responds.

The point is that, as you get better and better at generating great material, you can expect that others are going to want to engage with you. Some will simply pass along their thanks or kudos, but others are going to have questions, requests, and even conflicting opinions.

Regardless of whether you know the individuals commenting, and what you think of their opinions, it's a good idea to engage with them whenever possible. For one thing, creating an active discussion invites further feedback, which creates more "buzz" around your online content. For another, people are more likely to return if they see that their ideas are respected and responded to.

Most important, though, are the things you can learn from engaging readers and viewers. What they have to tell you could help you sharpen your marketing focus, develop new topics for the future, or even think about your content and ideas in new ways. In other words, they can help create a lot of inspiration going forward, while letting you build good business relationships at the same time.

Great content is too valuable to simply let it sit. So, after you've posted online, engage customers and colleagues to comment as often as possible.

Rule #9:
Invite Yourself to Someone Else's Party Once in a While

No matter what kind of customer you're trying to attract to your business website, there is a very good chance that there are already several other websites that they read and visit on a frequent basis. Sending some of your content to those sites (assuming they aren't owned by your competitors) can be a great way to build a following, create credibility, and generate those search-friendly backlinks that help you get found online.

This practice is often referred to as "guest posting," although that term has suffered a bit of abuse, like "content marketing" before it. Suffice it to say it works, and works very well, but only provided that you send out high-quality material that naturally makes readers and viewers more interested in what you're doing. Sending out generic fluff won't get it done.

The key to posting on other sites is to do your research. For one thing, you want to ensure that they have the kinds of visitors you want to draw into your business; otherwise, the effort you'll spend creating quality content for their site is wasted. And, you'll want to be sure that there is some mechanism (like an author resource box, a link at the end of an article, etc.) to invite potential customers to take the next step and visit your own site.

Beyond that, it can be hard to let some of your best material go. So, when you have a piece of content you really love, should you send it to someone else's site or keep it on your own? It probably depends on how well known you are in comparison to the other site. That's because your goal should be gathering new customers and creating a list of dedicated fans, readers, and followers... not just packing information with more keywords onto your own site.

Rule #10:
Remember That Great Content
Invites Links

Although "link abuse" has made it less important to have lots of sites pointing at your own for search engine optimization purposes, there are still reasons to build great backlinks. For one thing, Google does still count referrals from trusted websites (those with a good track record and a high page rank). And for another, having a link in the right place could generate lots of targeted traffic to your business website.

With that in mind, it's important to remember that a good content marketing plan can replace previous linking strategies. The more people in your industry see and get to know your content, the more they'll be inclined to link to it from their blogs and social profiles – especially if you're working with the kinds of strong, timely, and cutting-edge ideas we are encouraging you to develop.

For your part, it's important that you make your content easy to link to. How do you do that? By paying attention to things like titles and page lengths, URLs that are easy to paste, and content that's easy to quote or summarize. Additionally, you can include standard text or disclaimers (as we often do) that invite others to copy from or link to your pages, as long as they give you the appropriate credit.

Having a great content plan is the perfect way to attract backlinks, because they happen naturally, encourage readers to follow you, and bring your website closer to other high-quality sources of information. That means that you don't have to worry about back links for search engines, because they will eventually take care of themselves and make you a leader in the market.

Rule #11:
Build Your Content From
an Ongoing Plan

One of the toughest things about effective content marketing is coming up with a continual stream of interesting thoughts, ideas, and marketing pieces. As anyone who's ever faced a term paper on a deadline knows, it's incredibly difficult to sit down in front of a blank screen and generate pieces that are fresh and interesting day after day.

For that reason, it makes sense to do what the professionals do: work from an ongoing plan and calendar. Think of the team at your favorite magazine. We can guarantee, no matter what it is they cover, that they don't simply sit down a week before the issue is due and come up with a list of things to work on for the day. Instead, they have an ongoing schedule (or editorial calendar) of themes to work with, which then get expanded into related articles, topics, follow-ups, and so on.

You should do the same for your content marketing. Begin by deciding what kinds of topics your audience cares about, and how you can make those tie into your business or expertise. Then, think ahead and decide what sort of subjects to address, what kind of format you want for each one, when they'll need to be posted, and so on. By the time you're done with this process, you'll have an editorial calendar of your own that you can use to stay on track. It might take a bit of time and effort to devise, but believe us when we tell you that it's much easier (and more effective) than starting from scratch every week.

To make things even easier, get into the habit of keeping a file or notebook with spare ideas that occur to you. You'll be surprised at what kinds of thoughts can come to you in odd moments, and how you can use them to generate compelling content from one month to the next.

Rule #12:
The Best Inspiration Comes
From Several Different Sources

One of the strangest things about the information age is that, with more and more of it available online, we tend to get our information from fewer and fewer sources. That's largely a result of time and convenience, of course, but it's not necessarily a wonderful thing for your content marketing plan.

To truly think creatively and stand apart from your competitors, you need to be exposed to different thoughts and ideas. So, you can't be relying on the same kinds of websites, magazines, etc., as the businesses from which you are trying to differentiate yourself.

Besides, some of the best inspiration comes from "left field," so to speak. The more you read books (whether they are related to your business or not), talk to colleagues and customers, check out magazines, and generally get yourself thinking, the more likely you are to stumble upon a great idea for your next piece of content. The bottom line? Don't limit yourself to any one way of thinking, or to the same materials that everyone else is using.

And as we mentioned before, it's imperative that you have a way to capture these ideas when they come to you. Keeping a small notebook for quick outlines and ideas, and then copying them later into a word processor file, is a simple but effective way of organizing content marketing thoughts. The best inspiration can come from anywhere, at any time, and you don't want to let it slip away.

Rule #13:
Quality is as Important as Quantity

Although we have recommended that you stay on a regular editorial schedule for releasing content marketing pieces, don't let that confuse you – we certainly aren't advocating an assembly line approach. It's better to have fewer pieces of great content than lots and lots of poor ones posted to your site, blog, or social profiles.

This goes against the traditional thinking of the past, of course, where the emphasis was squarely on repetition, keyword-heavy articles, and an approach that basically boiled down to building a "content battering ram." But, keep in mind that the new approach to content marketing isn't about volume… it's about persuading people to check out your ideas and decide to engage with your business. You aren't necessarily going to do that with lots of content, but you can easily get there with great content.

So, take that time, energy, or money you would have put into creating huge amounts of writing and video and concentrate it into smaller pieces that are truly outstanding. Make ruthless editing a top priority.

When you post something online, make it so great that you feel like you're giving a gift to the world, not adding another brick to a wall of search engine material.

In the new era of findability and visibility, having lots of content doesn't count for much. However, producing a good deal of thought-provoking articles, posts, and clips on a regular basis is a sure way to stand out.

Rule #14:
Quantity Still Matters

As we hope you understand very clearly by now, content marketing isn't about producing endless numbers of articles, videos, and social updates in the hope that doing "more" will get you the right results. Search engines just don't work that way anymore, and the last thing customers want when they see junk is more junk.

But, you shouldn't take that to mean that you don't have to produce fresh content on a regular schedule. While quality is still more important, you'll never generate any momentum – much less lead-generation results – if you aren't putting fresh ideas out there on a regular basis.

So, that begs the question: How often is often enough? There isn't going to be a set answer that works for everyone, of course, but we recommend aiming for at least one piece of medium height and length, high-quality content per week. Very short blog posts or Facebook updates are certainly better than nothing, but don't really count for this requirement. What you want (at minimum) is an article, video, or other piece of content that takes someone at least a few minutes to read and process.

It can seem like the need for lots of content takes away the focus on quality, but in reality the opposite is normally true: The more often you are working on content for your marketing plan, the better it tends to be. Like everything, you improve with practice.

So, if you want to make the most of content marketing, concentrate on quality first, but make regular updates a big priority, as well.

Rule #15: Take Your Time

In the old days of "article marketing," website owners often hoped to boost their search engine rankings almost overnight. In the new world of content marketing, though, that's not going to happen – not only will Google and the other search engines want a bit of time to crawl your site and evaluate it, it's also going to take a while to develop a following on social media, attract readers to your blog, and build an online reputation.

Our advice? Take your time.

In one sense, this applies to individual pieces of content themselves. As we mentioned in the last section, you can't rush inspiration, and it's better to post nothing at all than it is to force something online, because you're only hurting your own credibility in the long term.

Bigger picture, taking your time is all about developing a plan, sticking with it, and trusting that the results will come. And they will. It might not happen as quickly as you would like, or hope, but if you're consistently releasing better content than your competitors, customers are going to find you and start listening. No matter what changes with the technical details of Google's algorithms, for example, or the Twitter interface, people are going to keep coming to the Internet and looking for answers for a very long time. Give out high-level advice and insight, and they'll start coming to you.

Success doesn't usually come quickly anymore, even on the Internet. But, if you're willing to take your time and commit to your content marketing plan, things are going to move steadily in the right direction until you reach a point where you start to dominate your market... and that can happen within just a few short months.

Rule #16:
Stop Buying Content From the Bargain Bin

Like so many things in the past couple of decades, the main components of the content marketing industry have largely been shipped overseas, or to the absolute lowest-cost providers. And, while that made a certain amount of sense when you were just looking for different ways to package keywords, it can absolutely kill your business now.

Although we certainly don't have a problem with people in developing countries trying to make a living, or writers, editors, and video producers who are just starting out in their craft, these aren't the types of entities you want crafting the public image for your company. Chances are, you wouldn't want them doing important sales and marketing work with your best customers, so why have them create content that's going to be associated with your company, and stored online, for years to come?

Now is the time to stop shopping in the bargain bin for content marketing pieces. You're much better served hiring someone who can communicate your sales points effectively (or taking the time to get them down in print and on video yourself) than you are trying to save a few dollars and losing your credibility with typos, factual errors, and other basic mistakes.

People will forgive a lot – including the occasional grammatical problem – if your content is honest, authentic, insightful, or even entertaining. But, being sloppy, a plagiarizer, or misinformed is the quickest way to put yourself out of business, and that's what you're going to get when you bypass the professionals and start getting your content from unreliable sources.

Rule #17:
Know Your Biggest Content Marketing Enemy

Want to know the one thing that will destroy your content marketing plan in a flash?

That's easy – being bland.

Not every idea has to be accompanied by sizzling headlines, lightning-fast jokes, and images that remind customers of a Las Vegas showroom. But, if you can't manage to use just a little bit of flair and showmanship, you're always going to run into problems. People are going to stop reading your blogs, your social updates are going to go unnoticed and unanswered, and the resources you commit to content marketing are going to be wasted.

Luckily, there are a few easy ways to dress up your content a bit. The first is to only engage in topics that you feel passionate about, or at least have strong interest in. It goes without saying that if you're bored with your content, everyone else is going to be, as well.

The second thing you can do is exercise a little bit of creativity. Never stop with "good enough" when another round of edits could make your content outstanding. Look for humor, excitement, or a controversial angle. These elements are always out there; they just aren't always easy to find.

And finally, if you don't have the time or talent to make your content outstanding, work with someone who does. Whether it's a full-service digital agency that can help you create themes and messages, or just an editor who can add a bit of spice to your social posts, go a little farther to ensure that your content is interesting to potential customers.

After all, your biggest enemy in content marketing isn't Google, your competitors, or even your budget… it's a disinterested buyer.

Rule #18:
Use One Piece of Content
to Promote Another

We've already mentioned why it's important to use content in a number of formats, and on a number of different sites, to create links, interest, etc. In a bigger sense, though, no piece of your content marketing plan should ever be on its own. That is, one article, post, or white paper should lead the viewer or reader to others.

The easiest way to accomplish this is through a clear and thoughtful navigation structure. You may have noticed that the best bloggers, for example, use keyword tags on their posts. This isn't just of interest to Google and the other search engines; it also makes it easier for readers who are interested in a particular topic to find other material that falls along the same lines. A number of more sophisticated, and more targeted, tools are available for your website that can help you do the same.

Another strategy is to support larger pieces of content with smaller ones. In other words, when you post a longer PDF document online, use smaller blog posts, Facebook articles, etc., on similar topics to get people interested. That way, you're adding to the overall effectiveness of the entire campaign, not just putting different pieces on the Internet and hoping for the best with each individual article or idea.

Rule #19:
Recycle Your Greatest Hits

The great thing about the ideas you come up with for content marketing is that they can often be used again and again. Earlier, we recommended that you put them into different formats so they are easier to find. It makes sense to bring up the "winners" once in a while, as well, just in case readers and followers missed them the first time around.

This is especially true as your content marketing plan gets bigger and stronger. The more new readers you are attracting, the more people you'll have who haven't seen some of your best work. So, by coming up with "reviews" or "roundups" at regular intervals, you can give bite-sized recaps of older content. It's a classic win-win situation all around: You get new material without having to brainstorm new ideas, the reader gets a great idea that they might not have seen, and linking back to the original piece can help you continue to build an even bigger following and reputation.

So how do you decide which ideas to bring back? That's easy – look at the ones that have attracted the most user comments, and then think about how they could be updated, summarized, or otherwise turned into a current topic. Additionally, you might want to consider pieces of content that had a great concept but didn't warrant that much attention, since you might be able to present them in a different way and create fresh interest.

Great ideas can live on and on. The trick, in content marketing, is to remember to come back to them once in a while and make the most of each one.

Rule #20:
Always Ask the Key Question
About a Piece of Content

Although we have spent a lot of time talking about "quality" and how it relates to content marketing, that's a difficult thing to define. Most of us know better content when we see it, but things are tougher when you're evaluating your own work – not to mention trying to keep producing new material on a regular schedule.

So, how can you decide whether your content is ready to be released? There is an easy way to tell: Ask yourself whether it's really worth the time someone spends after clicking on it.

Before you say "of course" and move on, think about things from a potential customer's perspective. Will they learn something valuable, be entertained, or at least come away with a new perspective and understanding on your topic? If the answer is "yes," then you've done a good job. If, on the other hand, the reader or viewer is going to get little more than a sales pitch, or if your ideas are hard to understand, then there is more work to do.

It's easy to violate this golden rule of content marketing, but taking shortcuts will always come back to haunt you. Once readers and buyers learn that they can't trust you with their time and attention, you'll have a hard time winning them back. But if you always give content that's worth their while, your plan will become more and more effective as you keep releasing new articles, videos, and social updates.

Rule #21:
Use Your Content to Turn Searchers, Readers, and Fans Into Buyers

At a certain point, you might find that content marketing stops becoming a chore and starts becoming a joy. Believe it or not, that isn't so unusual – experienced writers and artists will tell you that the process of creating, exploring ideas, and generating feedback can be addictive, much like exercise.

But, whether you learn to love it or not, your content marketing plan has one distinct job: to help the right customers find you and encourage them to take the next step. So, how do you use all of this information to make that happen?

The first step, as you probably realize by now, is having content that interests buyers and shows off your industry knowledge.

After that, include small calls to action within your content. Ask readers or viewers to take the next step by calling you, getting a free sample, signing up for your newsletter, or so on. Don't feel the need to go overboard. The point of content marketing is to interest potential buyers and let them take the next steps at their own pace. If your ideas are interesting and helpful, you'll continue to stand out online, and potential customers will keep finding their way back to you – and signaling their interest when they're ready to move forward.

That, as they say, is when the magic starts to happen. If your content marketing plan is strong enough, subscribers and followers will turn into new sales opportunities in greater numbers. Of course, you should have some kind of follow-up system in place to help the results and increase conversions, but once your plan is firing on all cylinders, the hard part is out of the way.

Where Are All the Tags, Keywords, and Technical Details?

If you're used to reading about traditional search engine optimization and online marketing, you might be wondering where all the technical details have gone in our plan. That is, why haven't we told you exactly where to put your tags, what specific keyword density you should be shooting for, or what the anchor text for your backlinks should look like?

We haven't shared that information, and won't, for three important reasons.

First, if you do want to get more technical, it's best to have a team of professionals help you. As we've mentioned, Google and the other search engines (not to mention social media sites) are always changing their algorithms and guidelines. That means what worked last month might be irrelevant or even harmful today; you want someone on your side who is watching the trends closely and can ensure that your plan stays up to date with the latest tactics.

Second, it just isn't that important. If you're working your content marketing plan the right way, you'll naturally get the results you're looking for. Ninety-five percent of what really constitutes good search engine optimization or social media marketing comes from having the right ideas expressed clearly and uniquely.

And finally, working with that other 5% takes a lot of time, energy, and expertise that might not pay off for your company.

As we're sure you realize by now, you are much better off with lots of great content that's attracting customers than you are with a few decent pieces that have been optimized to death. It's easy to drift back into that old mindset if you aren't careful, so don't lose the forest for the trees and wreck your great articles and posts by trying to find ways to fit in extra keywords, links, and other details that don't really matter.

A side note on Google Authorship for bloggers and webmasters alike. As authorship becomes a reality, 2014 is THE time to start building your online reputation the right way. Don't wait to set up rel:publisher and rel:author for your site.

Putting All the Pieces Together

Once you understand how content marketing is supposed to work, you'll be amazed at what a single blog post, video, or other piece can achieve. With just one great idea, you can literally open yourself up to thousands of new potential customers.

The real results come, however, when you start putting everything together – once you're releasing great pieces of content on a regular basis, distributing them around the Web, and using them to get buyers to take the next step and engage with your company. For a lot of businesses, this process builds like a forest fire. At first, there is a small spark, but it quickly spreads until it takes on a life of its own. When that happens, things like search engine optimization and social media marketing are secondary concerns. You're making the most of them, of course, but without having to target them directly.

That's where you want to be, and following the advice in this short e-book can get you there.

The flip side to this, naturally, is that content marketing takes a lot of work and creativity, especially in the beginning stages. Frankly, it takes more effort than most businesses are willing to put in. And so, even though they grasp the concept of content marketing, they try to cut corners and speed the process along. Before long, they are back to chasing Google algorithms and getting nowhere. At that point, they usually decide that the kinds of things we're talking about "just don't work," and jump onto the same Internet marketing treadmill that everyone else is running on.

But as difficult as content marketing might be, the results make it worth the trouble. Make content a priority for your business, and commit to trying it for at least six months (although a year would be preferable). Study this e-book, and scrutinize every blog post, tweet, video clip, etc., to make sure it falls in line with your marketing goals and quality standards. Do that, and the right results will come along. We know because we've seen it time and time again, and so have hundreds of other businesses.

The process works, but you can only get out of it what you put into it. So, shrug off your old ideas about SEO and Internet marketing, step into the content marketing age, and see what happens when you stop chasing equations and start using the power of effective communication to engage new customers!

One Final Word...

We're going to wrap this up by telling you something you already know: Creating great content isn't easy. It requires a certain amount of skill and talent, and even if you have those, you need time, inspiration, and (usually) a couple of aspirin close at hand.

For that reason, a lot of organizations turn to business web designers and digital agencies like ours to help them put their content plans into action. That's certainly a good idea, but don't simply hire someone and assume that everything will be handled for you.

Remember, it's your content, the future of your company that's at stake, and your reputation that's on the line. It goes without saying, then, that you should only work with the best. Don't accept anything less, and don't sit back and watch it all happen. Be engaged in the process. Even if you aren't writing the posts and shooting the videos, make sure it's your ideas that are driving the process forward.

The simple concepts in this short e-book can literally transform the way you attract customers, gather leads, or create sales opportunities over the Internet. But, whether you're creating your own content or having someone do it for you, the key to getting the right results is to look for long-term solutions and not quick-fix ideas.

We look forward to seeing your great content, and what you can achieve with it!

F

Hashtag: **#findability**

Educational assets:
   infographic: goo.gl/eHsG6b
   slide presentation: goo.gl/dTMrh

Get more:
   kayakonlinemarketing.com/blog

[1] Before search engines became so popular, Web directories assembled by actual people were widely used, but these have largely faded away in recent years. Besides, having people look at websites would slow the process down incredibly, given the huge number of pages being added to the Web every day.

Building a Better Business Website

10 Crucial Strategies for Turning Your Online Presence Into Something Your Company Can Actually Use

by Randy Milanovic

Why It's Time to
Start Thinking Differently
About Business Websites

Is your business website working as hard as it should be? Is it helping you to reach your real-world, bottom-line business goals?

Most aren't. In a day and age when it's possible to accomplish so much via the web, most business websites serve more as "web signs" than actual sources of new customers. They might have nice visuals, but they aren't compelling, or effective... and most certainly aren't generating new sales opportunities. Of course, most business owners and executives would love to have a stronger web presence, but aren't sure how to get one. Often, they fall into the trap of thinking that a different design, or perhaps the newest search engine optimization gimmick, will do the trick. That's understandable, but the reality is that it takes a lot of different pieces working together to produce a website that's actually good for your business.

In this short e-book, I am going to share ten of the most important strategies with you. These aren't

Randy Milanovic

just concepts or techniques that we've dreamed up over coffee, but proven tactics we have used again and again to produce extraordinary results. What kinds of results am I talking about? A 500% increase in new leads over a six-month time period hasn't been unusual, once we get all the components in place and working in harmony.

It's just as important to note that these aren't just new sales opportunities, but potentially better ones, with more lifetime value from each account. That's because, when new buyers are coming to you for answers and requesting information from your company rather than responding to your sales or advertising efforts, the relationship starts off on a better foot. There is more trust on both sides, with fewer negotiations over price, making it easier for a healthy long-term partnership to develop.

If that's the kind of performance you want from your business website, read on. You won't find any gimmicks or cheap tricks in the coming pages, but you will find simple, straightforward ideas that could dramatically change the way you think about your online presence....

About the author:

Randy Milanovic is a stage IV cancer survivor (having battled the Big "C" throughout the fall of 2009 and spring of 2010). At one point, having descended to the deepest depths imaginable, and reaching a place where the pain went away and his mind opened up with crystal clarity. Randy reports hearing his own voice boom through the darkness shouting... *"I haven't accomplished enough yet."*

Indeed, since his recovery from cancer, Randy has built a leading internet marketing firm, written two books, garnered international media coverage and watched his firm be nominated (and become a finalist) for **Small Business of the Year** to get just how motivated he is. Additionally, in late 2013, Randy became a BEST THINKER and weekly contributor to socialmediatoday.com, a leading North American blog site.

Building a Better Business Website

kayakonlinemarketing.com/publications

KAYAK Online Marketing Blog

kayakonlinemarketing.com/blog

EMA Toolkit
Worksheets

printed versions:

Enlarge 200% to fit
US letter size
worksheet.

.xls versions:

Download all 3, including the Editorial Lineup Worksheet at
kayakonlinemarketing.com/ema-toolkit

Landing Page(s) Worksheet	Topic & Title	Funnel Position (TOFU, MOFU, BOFU)	Primary Keywords
Project ID:			
Author:			
Due Date:			
Publish Date:			
Notes			

Sales & Marketing Funnel	Enlarge 200%	Marketing Qualified Offer(s)	
Marketing Persona	Activities	Awareness [TOFU]	Education [MOFU]
Identify decision-makers and influencers and focus content on them specifically.	Social Sharing, Engagement, Blog Posts & Comments, etc.	Free, non-sales information related to your services	Free non-sales info & introducti to YOUR related services

Made in the USA
Charleston, SC
06 February 2014